T0304472

Effusive Greetings to Friends

Also by Meighan L. Sharp

Anywhere You're Going (2016)

Also by David Huddle

My Surly Heart (2019)

Effusive Greetings to Friends

Meighan L. Sharp & David Huddle

groundhog
POETRY PRESS

2022

Library of Congress Control Number: 2022944235

ISBN: 978-0-9985685-1-5

Printed in the United States

Published by

Groundhog Poetry Press LLC

6915 Ardmore Drive

Roanoke, Virginia 24019-4403

www.groundhogpoetrypress.com

The groundhog logo is the registered trademark ™ of Groundhog
Poetry Press LLC.

For Hazel Hicks, who taught us so much.

Contents

Not Heaven, Just Death, Please

Ms. Hazel Hicks, 93, formerly of Fork Mountain,
arrived today in Purgatory, a bit ahead of schedule.

> August, the month of Hazel's birth,
> her parents carry the squirming,
> swaddled child to the porch

Ms. Hicks was preceded in her travels by brothers
and pets, parents and aunts, grandparents who'd talk

> only after dark to avoid the heat. Dizzy and warm
> with the sway and flush of night air,
> Hazel hears the careless scrape

of their over-worn shoes. She sends effusive
and apologetic greetings to friends, especially Zylphia,

> of the owl's call. Her mother nudges a nipple
> to Hazel's lips. When the rain blooms
> on the roof, her little fists unfurl;

as she recovers strength from witnessing
Ms. Hicks's collapse in the rock garden.

she loosens into sleep.

Ms. Hicks is known for her blight-free tomatoes
and her annual backyard dance at which

Hazel's mother dips and turns and coos;
the child absorbs the fearless
stumble and thrum,

nobody dances except drunks and children
and Ms. Hicks, who spins outrageously in the kitchen

sways through her mother's soft-moving
shoes. It's a dance, just for Hazel—
baby, strange one, dear—

while twilight rises and she refills the chip bowl.
Guests see her high-flung arms through the window,
she half awakes—

her shimmying shoulders. But, when Ms. Hicks steps
quietly back with food, only the drunks and children applaud.

I'm here, she creaks in unsettled cries.
Now what would you advise?

2

Ms. Hicks Didn't Even Realize There

was a wall like that until she'd
bashed her forehead & darn near
broken her nose on it a wall for
exhale & inhale eat & drink sleep
wake bathe dress wash the dishes
clean the house wash the clothes
pay the bills & taxes shovel snow
sweep the steps excrete urinate
menstruate nobody explained how
you did all these things & went
to bed & got up and started doing
them all over again until one day
she blacked out & came to slowly
to find she was standing on the
coffee table having kicked off all
its magazines & she was turning
in tight slow circles like a snow
queen in a snow globe singing *Old
MacDonald Had a Farm* but just the
first verse which was all she knew.

Messages

When you were under the fig tree, —Ms. Hicks stoops to read
four gold-leafed pages torn from a book—*I saw you.* She's losing

daylight. The rest of the text is gone. New to Purgatory,
Ms. Hicks walks the unfamiliar until the houses make her shiver.

She tries to decipher a lightning bolt on a red bottle cap,
a brass bullet casing. She has in mind thin trails between

untended side fences and viburnum bushes wide enough
for children to slide shoulder blades and ankles

and windmilling arms from one yard to the next. Sidewalks, not
shrub caves—that's where Ms. Hicks must direct her yearning feet.

Do you believe only because I told you I saw you under the fig tree?
We want to help Ms. Hicks, but she's still squinting for trash.

Wrangling the Recycle Bin

riles Ms. Hicks the hell up

activates the lengthy list

of ways she despises spending

her time stupid plastic items

pill bottles wine bottles

cardboard centers of paper

towels toilet paper evidence

she's devoted her life to

generating waste she can't

dodge the obvious we ruin

even the air we breathe every

swinging dick a phrase her

uncle Charlie savored made

to trash paradise Purgatory

whatever the hell it is uglify

even the blue heavens thank

science I never had children

she thinks but then wonders

if maybe she did and just

can't remember their names.

All Those Tiny Bits of Litter

A black steel batarang embedded
in the dirt by the half-dead maple
leaves Ms. Hicks feeling vulnerable.
It's not at all like a bottle cap
or some bin-blown recycling scrap
exposed between sidewalk seams, every
steady golden retriever stepping
serenely around it. The birds won't
come near this newly weaponized
backyard. Goldfinch tries to mitigate
the threat—perches on the birdbath, turns
her back. Ms. Hicks steps from a shrub,
widens gray eyes, breathes deeply, softens
the steel's sharpness to a smooth, cupped lump.

Ms. Hicks Makes a Correction

When the old man slips her a note,
I'm sorry for your lameness,
she steps out to confront him,
now kneeling in the dirt
by the dead maple. *Not lame!*
she shouts at him. *Merely*
imaginatively empowered,
she informs him. *You more than*
anyone else should understand
that. Get up, old man. Try to be
grateful for what is and what isn't.
The old man shifts on his knees,
kind of whimpers. *Can't I do*
that from down here? he whines.
Adamant Ms. Hicks quietly tells
him, *Certainly not. Get up now.*

Officials Look Into Erosion

Life had been enough—concrete and the occasional
shoring up of gas mains and storm drains. Fees
leveled on impervious surfaces
lent an air of progress, an air of concern.
Sinkholes were for archaeologists and
the ennuied operators of metal detectors.
Acupuncturists, puzzled by the loss
of clientele, slipped their needles between
sidewalk and lawn. Oh you lovelies, lovelies,
Ms. Hicks sings now as she pulls metal from grass,
punches thin tips to tomato-shaped pincushions,
her porcupines for sleepless nights. How they
feel together, clustered in the cup of her
palm, a subterranean distraction.

Doubts Her Own Mind Does

Ms. Hicks but doesn't let
it hold her back goes with
what she thinks as long as
it holds still but agile &
ready to cancel any former
thunk for the bright idea
just now occurring to her
the lady turns on a dime
as they say & who doesn't
like it's a rutabaga & if
anybody asks why the about
face she explains that she's
metaquizzical so there's no
why to her there's only yes
ma'am what can I do to help
you & by the way you're so
pretty I bet you've got
a million boyfriends.

We're a Destination Again

proclaims downtown Purgatory's newest

banner. Early morning and the street's

empty. Ms. Hicks peers at the sign, strung

between two lampposts. Perhaps *that's* why

she's here? She plops herself to the curb. *Ready*

to be finished, that was her life, or passing

time until she was—but not *this,* not

starting over here with no say-so,

no place for sleeping or memory, no

familiar drunks with routines, not even

irritatingly sociable neighbors to hide from

behind curtains. Even this town's banner

has given up yearning for a snappy

breeze. Ms. Hicks reclines on the sidewalk.

If Asked Politely Ms. Hicks Will

pose for a photograph though woe
be to any shutter-clicking fool
who tells her to smile she goes
into a rant about camels cobras
politicians chimpanzees donkeys
and the diminishment of integrity
mathematically linked to how many
times a human creature smiles to
curry favor or personally enrich
itself etcetera and so on believe
me you don't want to hear her go
off on the subject better to let
her enact her wacky poses lying
down stretched out on somebody's
lawn "Porpoise in Suburbia" she
calls it bowlegged up on tiptoe
winking squinting sticking out
her tongue "Annie Oakley Without
Her Guns," the photo ops Ms. Hicks
offers amateurs and pros alike stun
them into paralysis they've so
completely stepped into lalaland all
they can do is back away & plead
Oh no, Ms. Hicks please don't do
That. That's not necessary. Oh please.

In Purgatory, Seven Thousand Thrill-Seeking Daughters

stand over there—can't you see them? Fabulously

underwrought, they're lounging on curbs, vaping

last week's flavors. Hand-painted, recycled

aluminum feathers jazz-hand from their backs,

topple their posture like old books. Behind

the Emporium, the aunts' lamentations

and plans filter through actual tobacco

smoke, season crates of rotting cantaloupe.

Bitter Ms. Hicks pokes pebbled skin with an

arthritic knuckle—surely she made good use

of her hyped-up existence. Tomatoes,

azaleas, *microbrews!* There's something

to flutter on the back of a tongue. Bitter

Ms. Hicks palms the fruit. Aims. Fires.

Ms. Hicks Avoids the Old Goat

as best she can without going out
of her way he's pleasant enough &
he flatters her which no one else
does & truth is she's susceptible

to his witty way of complimenting
her but he's ancient deaf & won't
get a hearing aid & stares at her
mouth trying to read her lips but

still stupidly misunderstands her
once he heard her say *Mary Stuart*
instead of *They're not very smart*
they were talking about Tea Party

Republicans & his eyes brightened
as if she'd brought up a favorite
historical figure & he pronounced
her name as if she was his adored

dead mother *Unfortunately* he said
the dear lady was easily besotted
& got herself married three times
before Elizabeth finally…. Stop!

Ms. Hicks shouted loud enough for
the old goat to hear her it might
have been the first word that had
gotten through to him in a decade

& Ms. Hicks was shaken by the way
she'd discombobulated him his lip
actually trembled & he blinked as
if he might cry too but that word

besotted kept riling her up *Don't*
talk to me about a woman's desire
turning her into a fool women put
up with besotted men because they

respect desire know it's evidence
of a human being but if any woman
truly follows her heart men start
saying she's so unfortunate —Ms.

Hicks had to stop herself because
she knew she'd always thought her
own heart was an idiot she'd been
careful never to let that drummer

march her into battle or make her
do something risky. They were out
in broad daylight beside Leunig's
facing each other blinking & each

of them clearly upset & wondering
how they'd locked themselves into
this situation Ms. Hicks saw that
the old goat was afraid which she

liked but just then she wanted to
teleport herself home where she'd
go to bed & curl up with her head
under the covers & she opened her

mouth to say *Please excuse me but
I have to*—But that was when he
touched her elbow & said *I always
admired Mary Stuart I'm sorry for*

*saying she was besotted I used to
dream I saved her. A boy has that
kind of dream you know.* Ms. Hicks
didn't know & couldn't think what

to say so she willed a smile onto
her face which probably horrified
the old coot & said *I forgive you*
which was only approximately true.

Driver Displays Stupidity

Some days Ms. Hicks believes nowhere is far
enough away. Across her street, a man
hisses at his spouse as they start the morning
carpool, *What are you going to do? Ground me?*
And their little girl carries a 1959 copy
of *The Longest Day*. The truth is, she tells
her parents, Rommel returned to Germany
on June 6th to celebrate his wife's birthday.
Ms. Hicks hears the girl say, above her parents'
silence, *I'm glad I read this book.*
The girl's parents won't look at each other.
At the corner, the wife applies the brake
a little too firmly. Ms. Hicks removes
another batch of needles from the grass.

Not Much Fazes Ms. Hicks

but the graceful young man
in skin-tight running gear
jogging backward uphill
as she walks down kicks
up with his little dance-
like steps a mayhem in her
chest the equivalent of a small
drone touching down beside
her kitchen sink so muscular
and sturdy he startles her
his grim face concentrating
out toward the distant lake
he'd butt first run over her
except she swerves aside for
which he rewards her with
utter disregard touching
Ms. Hicks's untouchable heart
like a surgeon's finger testing
for life ever so briefly.

What if You Are Honest

in everything, Ms. Hicks thinks, except one small thing?
A wrapper of dishonesty wadded and tossed
in a dovetailed drawer that sticks each time it's opened.

Ms. Hicks reaches her hand to the back
of her mother's dresser and pinches the wrapper with two
fingers, slides it to the front, smooths

the paper's permanent creases to see one version of her story
pressed out again before her. We see her contemplate
the recycling bin. We see her memorize a journey to the landfill.

Ms. Hicks tears and chews bits of untruth
like an operative in the Eastern bloc. She straightens
her sunglasses. Adjusts her collar. Hunches her shoulders.
Dead-drops the spittled paper back in the drawer.

Ms. Hicks Gets a Trumpet FedExed

to her front door *Present for you*
says the note that comes with it
To replace that old trumpet you
played in high school and I broke
Maybe now you can forgive me no
signature & Ms. Hicks can find
neither a name nor an address
bemused she extracts the horn
from its case waggles its valves
sits with it turned up on her lap
the way they did in band practice
she remembers the girl who snatched
her old trumpet & cracked it across
her knee like a stick of kindling
then she handed it back & smiled
at Hazel as they called her then
& walked away Ms. Hicks can't
remember why the girl did it she's
not about to put this mouthpiece
to her lips she sits very still
& holds the horn correctly
I forgive you Ronnie or Bonnie
she whispers *Whatever your name was.*

Ms. Forgiveness

Sap-fingered, tree-climbing girl no one else will
touch branch-balances to spyglass her domain.

Kids on the bus crick their necks to find her,
concealed among the leaves. When she catches

their eyes, nods, nine-year-olds straighten spines,
breathe deep, remember she'll come to them

in late-life dreams, banish sleeplessness
and frost. *You did fine,* she'll say. *Not to worry.*

You don't ride the bus? She's there for you, too—
teetering on fence rails, house eaves, dervish

spinning through leaves. If you think you can't
find her, just lean against the lowest branch.

Any tree. She'll sense your tremoring
breath, rain acorns to wake you.

Between Ms. Hicks & Her Body

a psychodrama goes on the ordinary
person couldn't possibly grasp but
Ms. Hicks is used to it & becomes
energized on days of conflict which
is to say most days that begin with
her body having waked her four or five
times with leg cramps thirst blocked
sinus bladder panic snoring rotten
mouth the nightmare of Aunt Mary Alice
switching her legs again diarrhea
or gas or both *Good morning, Traitor,*
she will tell it when she gives up
on sleep for good *Thank you for yet*
another night of bedtime hell I
can't wait to drag you down into
into the grave with me but truth be
told Ms. Hicks mostly cares for her body
as one cares for a bullying older sister
when springtime arrives & Ms. Hicks
receives a whiff of lilacs or a soft
evening breeze prickles up some goose
bumps on her arms or when she mows
her grass & slips off her shoes to
walk on it or when she sprinkles sugar

on a heaping bowl of strawberries & eats

the whole thing or when she hears James

Brown yelp *Hunh!* and gets down with him

doing steps & flinging her hips around

in her kitchen or even when godless

heathen that she is she sneaks into

the late afternoon empty Episcopal

Cathedral downtown & sits by herself

in the high vaulted dimming light Oh

Lordy why then Ms. Hicks tears up so

pleasured she can hardly stand it she

knows perfectly well she doesn't deserve

a fine & delicate instrument like this flesh

demon she's lived in all these years this

hateful thing that in her sleep tonight

won't hesitate to give her aching knees

or hiccups just to remind her of the idiot

heart that goes thump-thump-thump in her chest.

They Won't Nix Death

Ms. Hicks purses her lips, closes her eyes,

refuses to say thank you, though one suspects

she's pleased. Wouldn't matter anyway since

Ms. Hicks would just mouth the words

at an empty street, at a May basket

dropped on her porch, overflowing with freshly

cut, dark pink azaleas. Sprigs—they won't nix

death. A winter-hatted-in-spring boy

on a green bike meets her eyes, extends

his arm, points at departing nothing. As if

she's spoken, as if she's desperate to know

the flower bearers! Phantom girls, maybe—

giddy with their charity and muscled

legs. Oh. They run with lung-burn and smoke.

Ms. Hicks in Spring Again

Ms. Hicks's eyes, they say, are the confused
color of pigeon necks; thus, we are thankful
whenever she closes them, a mercy for us,
though she perhaps intends an insult. As for
departing nothing, that issue has yet to be
settled. One of those phantom girls (as you
call them) once ran all the way to the end
of where the spring boy pointed and found lo
and behold a wren's nest in an old shed, the bird
rattling the shack with her song. Of course the girl
ran back to tell us and did so, babbling with passion
and even a note or two of the song itself. When we
turned to eavesdropping Ms. Hicks, she shook
her head and closed her eyes even tighter.

Most People Should Take a Deep Breath

and just shut their lovely lips. *Catch a bubble in your mouth—*
said Ms. Hicks's first grade teacher as they'd roam
the wide, light halls, six-year-olds puckered up
serious and silent as cartoon blowfish.
Hazel unbubbled her mouth. Didn't speak.
Straightened her sweater but refused hair ribbons.
Why call attention? The people she wanted
as friends would find her anyway. Her pals
would understand one raised eyebrow,
the code of her tilted head. Her pals
might stare one moment longer—and get it
all. Afternoons she reads alone on the couch
or kicks a ball without so much as a hum—
others on some common frequency
ride their bikes to find her.

Why Ms. Hicks Neither Wastes Nor Minces

Words for some reason in her childhood
took on tangibility they were things
you could actually taste like sand
from the beach you put in your mouth
before your mother reamed it out and
told you not to do that again or books
you could get your Uncle Phillip to
read to you if you asked nicely and
chose the caboose book his favorite he
read so expressively toddler Ms. Hicks
loved him and sat on his lap touching
the pages though he drank too much and
her father said he wasn't a very nice
person or Legos you could put together
in a tower your brothers liked to knock
down or Pink Baby who didn't cry if you
carried her upside down or by her foot
and who helped you take naps or Spotty
the rocking horse who sometimes tipped
over or the musical vacuum cleaner you
could run with through the whole house
and sometimes change into a lawn mower
words could change a dining room table

into a caboose or a cave to hide in or

a jail your brothers could lock you up

in if you really liked words they lived

in your brain and belonged to you you

could do secret things with them and

it was okay for somebody else to play

with them you had to share even though

you didn't like sharing but it could be

okay if the other kid understood they were

your words and they couldn't take them

home with them they had to give them back.

Seven-Year-Old Hazel Memorizes

all the names. Each door has at least one,

some two, roommates or spouses living out

their last years in the veneer of home.

With a wave of her hand, she disappears

from the reception desk, a tagless guest,

follows *Green Caped Walker Lady, Near*

Sighted Bird-Nose Man, marks strangers in her life

list until she reaches their true nests

and names, hides behind greenly fake ficus

trees to guess which doors they'll enter.   We trust

Hazel's instincts, her belief that counting

matters. If they see her watching, they fuss

over her a little—*Who are you visiting,*

my dear? She holds up her book in her fists.

Ms. Hicks Recalls the Goat's Milk Episode

Famous or infamous in her family was when her grandmother tricked her into trying goat's milk. This was long before Ms. Hicks became Ms. Hicks, she was just Hazel or Little Hazel as her father liked to call her six-or-seven-year-old self. Her ancient grandmother was in a nursing home and in a wheelchair. She smelled like a bathroom, and Little Hazel hated going to visit her. But the grandmother was fixated on the child. *She's just like me, look at her nose, look at her mouth,* she rasped. The grandmother still subscribed to *Prevention Magazine* and got it into her mind that Little Hazel had to drink goat's milk, which she had especially delivered to the nursing home just for her. Ms. Hicks recalls the conversations with her grandmother that were like torture sessions. Always she refused the goat's milk because growing up to be like her grandmother was worse than anything she could imagine. *Just try it,* was her grandmother's refrain. She had this witchy smile for Hazel whenever she said it. The grandmother bribed and cajoled and threatened and bullied, but Little Hazel pretended she was a rock and sat still with her eyes and her mouth clamped shut. The grandmother was old and crazy but she wasn't stupid. *Just try it and you won't have to come see me any more.* Little Hazel wasn't stupid either. She knew right away this could be a really good deal if the goat's milk didn't kill her. She opened her eyes and her mouth, stood up, accepted the cup her grandmother offered, held her breath, brought it to her mouth, took a sip, dropped the cup, and spat the milk on the floor. *You didn't try it!* the old lady shouted from her wheel chair. Her face was the scariest Hazel had ever seen. *I did try it, look at my tongue,* said the child, sticking her tongue out. *I tried it and it tasted like pig snot.* That was the end of Little Hazel's visits to the nursing home. She never found out what the grandmother told her parents, but they never again tried to make her go. Nor, when she was twelve, did they try to make her attend the grandmother's funeral. In the family they joked about it more and more as Little Hazel grew up to be Ms. Hicks. The child didn't mind the joking; she knew it was just a way they could talk to make it feel all right for them. For her it was already all right. She had been the only other person in that room when her grandmother tried to poison her, and she'd done what she had to do. She wasn't scarred by it as far as she knows. As a grown-up Ms. Hicks likes goats and laughs at pictures and videos of them. That way their eyes make them look like they're crazy animals and pretty darned happy being exactly that.

Ms. Hicks Considers Staying

She could grow to love

Purgatory's plush

nothingness—movie

theater seating,

a big empty screen,

butter but no popcorn.

Here she could grow

nine elegant heads

without drawing

attention. *Tension*

is for the living—

some precocious bat-

winged girl says sweetly

from her unsweet dreams.

Ms. Hicks thinks, *yes but*

suspects she is one

half of a typed, two-

part punctuation

mark (a cupped hand

(a bent body waiting

Before Swallows Flew Into Ms. Hicks's

summer camp classroom Hazel Hicks knew

herself to be a child like other children

as ants know they are like other ants &

it was so hot that day Miss Childress

propped the door open hoping for cool air

but what she got was two barn swallows

swooping into the room *like little souls*

frantic to find the bodies they'd fallen

from Ms. Hicks thinks now that the memory

has her in its spell & the children put

their hands over their heads & squealed

while the birds rocketed against the wall

of windows but Miss Childress sat calmly

& watched the creatures a little crooked

smile on her face which was probably what

freed Hazel not to be afraid as the other

children were but to sit still even though

excitement and pleasure kept ricocheting

through her body & Miss Childress wanted

her help & they both felt something those

others couldn't feel & when Miss Childress

stood up slowly so as not to panic the birds

even more Hazel stood up too & moved with

Miss Childress toward the windows against

which the swallows flung themselves & flapped

their pointy little wings & Miss Childress

raised her hands toward one & Hazel raised

her hands toward the other & they kept

moving slowly & calmly Hazel knowing to do

just what her teacher was doing—*She was*
only 16 then Ms. Hicks thinks now *Not that*
much older than I was—Hazel was 9 & this
was the wildest moment of her life & yet
she & her teacher were moving so slowly &
carefully it was like a dream & Hazel was
the first to trap a swallow down in the
lower corner of the window and catch it
in her hands—*Yes, she did that!*—then
Miss Childress caught the other one & she
carried hers to the table to show the other
children & Hazel followed her the little
birds' heads sticking up out of their cupped
hands the other children put their faces
right up to the birds' heads & Hazel felt
that swallow's heart thrumming in her palms
& she followed Miss Childress outside into
the heat & light & they looked at each other
& Miss Childress had that crooked grin on
her face & Hazel felt her own face smiling
& they put their cupped hands close to each
other so that the birds' beaks almost touched
& Miss Childress raised her eyes to the sky
just a split second & whispered "On three" & she
counted & they lifted their hands & opened
their palms up & Miss Childress shouted "Go!"
& the swallows zoomed up & out into the light
& Hazel Hicks may not have understood exactly
what had happened to her in those minutes but
—& Ms. Hicks still feels it in her body—
that was the instant that child became herself.

Running with Eggs

Are these ones ok? Eleven-year-old Hazel asks her mother one Saturday morning, offering up a smooth brown oval on each palm before she slips them in her coat pockets and turns toward the woods. Her mother calls out to Hazel's back *careful don't break them in your clothes careful don't drop them I'm not giving you more so don't use them til you're ready careful don't let anyone see you careful!* Hazel hears her right foot say *yes* and her left foot say *ma'am*

yes   *ma'am*   *yes*   *ma'am*   *yes*
                ma'am

                                                yes ma'am yes'm and she's breathless

at the place where the concrete sidewalk drops off and the trees and dirt soften everything so she can't hear her feet speaking. Instead, she listens to the eggs lightly lifting and settling with each stride, sliding against the lining of her red coat: *careful careful careful.*

She slows her pace, slips hands in pockets *don'tbreak don't break don't
                break   don't*—until she stops raises the left egg to daylight sits with it awhile strokes the shell with her thumb sets it in the root nest of the poplar—   *break.*

Brothers Is Who Ms. Hicks Holds

responsible for her turning out
so impossible not that she'd
wish she was some other way but
a boy on either side of a girl
child means she gets squished &
shoved by the one while she's
half mothering the other both
of them busy as chimpanzees on
a tilt-a-whirl looking for ways
to fall off something or crawl
into the dishwasher or scald
their faces off but those two
hoodlums were never happier than
when pulling her hair twisting
her nose getting her lost hiding
her babies mocking her begging
her not to tell on them while
they told complete lies on her
Ms. Hicks thinks boys get born
busy & needing to kick throw
poke or smack something whereas
she'd have turned out sweet as
chocolate pie if Tommy and Jack
hadn't turned her whole childhood

into airborne ranger training
for toddlers they made her tough
that's what those two did & she
can't work up much regret about it
even now when she sees a one-year-
old napping so immaculate & mild
its eyelids fluttering its little
mouth puckering & making those
kissy grunts & squeaks she gets
a burning urge to pinch its fat
arm to watch it open & widen its
eyes & hear it shriek like it's
being put to death & then she
Hazel Hicks survivor of brother
torture knows just how to glide
out of that room find its mother
& murmur with impeccable innocence
Wonder what's wrong with the baby.

Power Outage

Our hero fumbles
for the light as if
she's freshly wakened—
August left late Sunday

night and forgot to call
its replacement.
Lantern's in the basement—

dumb place for it. She's new
at this, knows she must
climb over dark piled
in the room's middle

like a tipped box
of remaindered books.
Board corners nick

her shins, bleed her knees.
She's dreaming. A lost,
stumbling man can't stop
climbing concrete stairs.

She takes his shaking arm.
Where's the damn door?
Just keep going, Ms. Hicks

mutters back at him.
She's pleading, really,
bends her head, palms
her eyes. Her body's

still whole, even if
she cannot see it.

Spoken or Written the Word *Love*

puts Ms. Hicks in a swivet of nostalgia

& rage—on the one hand Lucy Beth Grosclose

whose tight pigtails and gentle ways

in first grade unleashed such adoration

in Hazel Hicks she may still be in recovery

when they haul her away to the nursing home

but on the other hand Danny Surratt whose poor

hygiene & shiny face littered with zits

she'd hardly noticed until that day near the end

of their junior year of high school she overheard

him say the word *slut* to his pal Eugene & though

he'd finally got her to tell him she loved him

she'd never even let him slide his hand under

her bra & so she swung her book bag into his back

& kicked his legs out from under him then

kicked him in the ribs when he fell down right

outside their homeroom. Miss Bryant sent

Hazel Hicks to the principal's office

where she shed no tears & did not flinch

when Mr. Whitt explained how she should know

they could put her in jail for what she'd done
to Danny. She tightened her jaw and kept her
silence because she knew she'd assaulted Danny
only out of sadness for Lucy Beth having moved

with her family to Cleveland eight years ago &
never a word heard from her since then. Even now
remembering how softly the two of them talked this
fiery mix of wrath & tenderness rises in Ms. Hicks.

Yes, they were just children and so it never
occurred to either of them to say it or even
to think it but that doesn't stop Ms. Hicks
from wishing they'd had that word between them.

Woman Stops for Ducks

Twelve's the current count of mallards—
middling age, Ms. Hicks would say,
an age she recalls but not with any fondness.

Fourteen was how they started, fuzzy
things tripping over each other and their mother—
incompetently underfoot.

Six weeks later, two are gone,
a heron or cat—who remembers now?
Ms. Hicks fills her pockets with dried corn

(two handfuls) and sets out each afternoon
to lure those left to the fence near the pond
just so she can count twelve beaks

coming at her in a straight line—
easier than reading obituaries.

Of the Words Ms. Hicks Considers

harmful to her health foremost is

probably *Cute* which makes her grit

her teeth or in some pronunciations

makes her actually spit whether

she's indoors or out but then

there's *Share* which makes her go

all pukey in the gut *Wonderful* &

Interesting are on her list as

constipation-causers one time after

she'd listened to a cooking program

on NPR she couldn't poop for a week

Incredible and *Amazing* amp up her death

wish *Lifestyle* and *Patriotic* make her

short of breath *Fun* gives her a headache

or makes her sneeze rapidly *Healthy*

isn't so bad except it makes her gassy

Special makes her want to head-butt

whoever said it but the one she thinks

will eventually kill her is *Enjoy* next

time some pretty-faced waiter sets

a plate of food in front of her &

sweetly chirps *Enjoy* like a tweeted

sound-byte from the kitchen Ms. Hicks

is going to will herself into having

a seizure falling down kicking chairs

& tables twitching drooling swallowing

her tongue & maybe that will teach them

to think twice before commanding a person

like herself to *Enjoy* her house salad

a person who used to enjoy actually

conversing with other human beings.

Ms. Hicks Does Not Believe

in *old*'s fulcrum

but attempts to find

it anyway. Was it the year

washing her own hair

became too much

trouble? Or the year

she burned all files

with her fall leaves—

snapshots missing

labels, her dead

sister's record

of birth, her first

grade diary,

ephemera

loosed from pages

in one sharp shake

over the flames?

Her life's

going up around her—

gorgeous smoke hair

ash bones, the dirt-

smudged child she was

hunched over

a page, penciling

and scratching out

her misspelled future

*destinashun*s.

                    Oh, but

here, in this new place,

Ms. Hicks gives up

longing; when it

appears she smacks

it in the face.

We see her now,

at the playground

with her socket

wrench, bending

to dismantle the seesaw.

Ms. Hicks Appreciates Certain Kinds

of heavy trucks snow plows that roar
into her city's neighborhoods hours
before daylight & turn the streets
into smooth channels to work & school

dark brutal monsters called out of
hiding from caves by the falling snow
festooned with blinking lights &
clattering rapidly & raising white

plumes above slanted scraping blades
their drivers nearly invisible men
of clear purpose Ms. Hicks imagines with
thermoses by their sides & wives

still asleep in their beds at home.
Ms. Hicks also admires the concrete
mixers operated by J. D. Ireland
Construction Company powerful trucks

that transport wet cement in twirling
cauldrons shaped like the back ends
of giant bumble bees clover-green ogres
that on St. Patrick's Day drive all

over town draped in green ribbons

& bows blatting their thunderous horns

that startle & irritate the citizens

until they realize it's the Ireland

truckers celebrating St. Paddy. Ms. Hicks's

two-year-old nephew has his own book

of trucks that make their particular horn

noises when you press that truck's picture

& Ms. Hicks who can hardly bear most

things mechanical & loud & polluting

because of that boy who carries his

truck book to her & climbs on her lap

& asks her to read to him Ms. Hicks

who is no soft-hearted baby talker

sweetie of an aunt does what he asks

again and again & when she witnesses

one of those trucks ripping through town

like it's been dispatched straight

out of Hell Ms. Hicks the committed

pedestrian raises her fist & pumps it.

After the Incident

with a wild boar, we are skeptical of Ms. Hicks and her incidents. When she says, over and over again, *bereft*, we can't think what she might mean. Her doorframes seem solid. Her sashes latch appropriately. Her storm windows distract the cold. Most of us agree the zinnias shading the shed's south side are the first fireworks we see in July. In the fall, when she's on her roof checking shingles and cleaning gutters, no one steps across the lawn to steady the ladder for her descent. Ms. Hicks's competence leaves us with empty hands and mouths.

Ms. Hicks tells us she found the wild boar (which we all agree was likely somebody's escaped pig) knocking around her living room one night. *How*, we ask, *did it get in?* Those of us who knew her as a child might say, to lure her attention, *Hazel?* The damage is clear—feathers from torn sofa cushions snow her floor, books have abandoned the shelves, low (are those *tusk*-scrapes?) scratches mar her cabinets. *Hazel? Hazel?* We don't dare touch her. The back door is open wide and Ms. Hicks stands with one hand on the frame, gazing into the yard as if something's been lost. *Oh*, she tells us, *I let it in.*

Christmas Songs Bludgeon Ms. Hicks

while she's in the doctor's office
receiving photodynamic therapy
for her face's romance with melanoma

Beyoncé Elvis Bing Crosby Pentatonix
Dolly Parton Nat King Cole Liberace
The Pogues Louis Armstrong relentlessly

batter Ms. Hicks's ears & brain while
she sits embraced in purple-white light
from a machine heating up her poor face

parboiling it she's ready to say if
anyone inquires where she got that
sunburn but it feels like Rudolph

& sleigh bells & fricking Santa Claus &
jingle bells & the little drummer boy
& the herald angels are unraveling what

few wits she has left at least cancer
doesn't try to put her in a mood to go
shopping Ms. Hicks grits her teeth

against the onslaught it's a battle
she thinks her iron souled self versus
the baby Jesus & suddenly she's won—

the procedure's over they tell her to
go wash her face they send her home
with salves & pamphlets & it's snowing

in the parking lot but she's free never
to hear another Christmas song as long
as she lives which she hopes won't be

all that long but then in her own house
her own kitchen she hears voices laughing
& glances out the window over her sink

where next door are two college students
a boy & girl scraping up snow to build
a fat-bellied snowman these youngsters

are sculpting up a big brainless snow blob
they'll no doubt put a hat on stick a carrot
into its face & figure out some idiotic

way to make it smile inanely through her
window those kids are out there are tossing

soft snowballs at each other & flirting

she'd open the window & yell at them except
she can't think of what words she could shout
that would heal her burning face her abused

ears her holiday waterboarded spirit the ruined
world her certainty she's become somebody even
the baby Jesus can't love any more Ms. Hicks

Ms. Hicks are you there can you hear me?

Children Appear

Parents wish it were otherwise, yet kids
rise from Ms. Hicks's shrubbery like delicate
mosquitoes whining at twilight. She's startled
by their shadows, the places they perch. Eyes

cupped, she searches the caved boxwood,
the runneled channels between houses,
eave-shrouded and dank. A hooded head
hunches in the birdbath! Flowered jeans flat-flank

the orange shed! One dark-mouthed child blows
an *O* against the greenhouse glass, finger
webs Ms. Hicks's frizzed hair and floats a flip-turn
back to the others. Hazel's ribcage expands:

longing swept away by the swarm. If she closes
her eyes, she senses them hovering or maybe
propping her upright. Five or five thousand—
blurred by the night, we know she welcomes them all.

Ms. Hicks Realizes Effigies

please her though their art
or lack of art doesn't much
matter it's their stoniness
she likes granite or marble
she prefers heroic athletes
males with rounded buttocks
worthy of Percherons female
sweeties who modestly cover
virginal breasts and nether
regions or perhaps posed as
archers but Ms. Hicks turns
ecstatically silly when she
encounters stone alligators
turtles or even bunnies she
has been heard confiding in
them or beseeching whatever
deity it is that looks over
them *O please let me be one*
of you make my next life be
brainless and still give me
a garden fountain old trees
shade some grass and a very
few visitors to smile at me
before going somewhere else.

No, Thinks Ms. Hicks. Or Maybe, Yes.

Even though she doesn't believe in glorious
resurrection, Ms. Hicks half-prays, admires
river rocks, stray sticks, palm-sized pieces

of moss peeled from dirt in one place and rooted
still-living in another. She conjures
the body of a woman unearthed from fifty years

of restless sleep, reconstructs her free of charge
as a Bot Shafer tango dancer, spangle-costumed,
something new in Purgatorial courtesies. Even now,

she's being sought, her features obscured
by tape and cloth. This body—a woman unearthed
by a stray spade on Chestnut Street—will rise

shaking to the roof, an unsteady kite with a tail
made from 120 girls' dresses, tied arm
to arm, the owners' identities unknown.

One Time Ms. Hicks Saw Somebody Die

It wasn't anybody she was close to
or knew very well it was her Aunt
Wilma Ransom an old maid they said
she was & she'd asked the family
to let her come do her dying with
her own people she wasn't particular
which ones took her home just didn't
want to have to die with strangers
being paid to watch her do it.
                              Ms.
Hicks was thirteen difficult even
for herself to live with a pouter
of colossal intensity her mother
called her hoping some wry diction
would make the child more bearable
it didn't it was then her brothers
stopped calling her Hazel they said
she wasn't that sweet little girl
any more not that that was ever
                              what
she was but she & Aunt Wilma had
got along all right the three or
four times the lady had visited
over the years & so Ms. Hicks didn't

object when her father suggested

she take on the death watch a.k.a.

the task of tending to Aunt Wilma

during the weeks of her attempt at

making a graceful exit Ms.

                                       Hicks

didn't confess to them that death

& Aunt Wilma & Elvis were all she

could find in the world to respect

in those days & she worried that

Elvis might crumble under too much

scrutiny she thought it worth her

while to cozy up to the old lady &

to death mostly just to find out if

the ten thousand lies of school

                                       &

family dinner & church & manners

& building character & hygiene &

everything in moderation & getting

a good night's sleep & President

Reagan & zippity doo-dah etc. applied

to them she was pretty sure death

was rock solid in its integrity

but she worried Aunt Wilma might

reveal churchy inclinations

                              she'd

hidden back when she & Hazel had
enjoyed iced tea & swinging on
the back porch glider together &
Aunt Wilma had invited Hazel to
play her trumpet for her several
times & Hazel was just learning &
wasn't all that far beyond scales
& Old MacDonald but Aunt Wilma
smiled listened with her head

cocked

& rocked the glider with her feet
while Hazel stood in front of her
& performed her recital piece it
would make Ms. Hicks cringe now
because it must have sounded like
Satan was her trumpet teacher but
Aunt Wilma talked to her like she
was almost a grown-up & said it
was funny about practicing if

you

kept at it you got better whether
you wanted to or not & then the
old lady told her about taking
piano lessons when she was a girl
& how she hated it until one day
she didn't mean to but it turned

out she loved three or four bars
of a Russian peasant dance she was
trying to learn for her recital

It

made me cry she told Hazel *but it*
was the sweetest crying like the
music had just announced to me
that I could make this beautiful
sound—it was in A-major I remember
that—any time I wanted to & Aunt
Wilma trailed off then but Ms. Hicks
had it in her mind & kept it there
like a bracelet or a locket

hidden

in her underwear drawer & so when
Aunt Wilma Ransom arrived at the
Hicks's house driven there by her
cousin Stanley in his new maroon
Buick Ms. Hicks came out to help
her move in & right away the old
lady looked her over & didn't quite
manage a smile but nevertheless the
two of them let each other know

they

remembered the other & those iced
tea afternoons on the back porch &

Ms. Hicks felt like her heart had

shifted in her chest so she carried

one of the suitcases while Stanley

& her father carried the old lady

into the house between them even

though they said she didn't weigh

enough to make it a two-man job

                                but

that's how they did it anyway &

somehow Aunt Wilma made Ms. Hicks

understand she was half amused &

half humiliated by the spectacle

she & the men were making she asked

them very softly please not to show

her sit-downer as they ever so

awkwardly carried her up the porch

steps & Ms. Hicks stepped close

                        &

told her she'd hold onto her robe

& keep anything from showing & so

that's how it was with them in the

days to come Ms. Hicks ceased her

pouting even around her brothers &

the family let her be the boss of

how things were to go with Aunt

Wilma's dying & it was as if a new

& improved human girl had

                    dropped

into Hazel Hicks's body & as Ms.

Hicks thinks about it these many

years later she sees it as a time

when her life took on an intensity

she might never have known if not

for Aunt Wilma & the dwindling of

her spirit her breath her ability

to move or speak & yet—Ms. Hicks

sees it now—they had such a

                    complete

understanding of each other that

actually speaking aloud would have

been a come-down from what they

could manage by moving their eyes

their lips their eyebrows Aunt

Wilma became her out-of-the-body

instructor or maybe she was her

in-the-body instructor because so

much of what Ms. Hicks had to do

                    was

to appease Aunt Wilma's body from

which the old lady felt somewhat

bemusedly detached as if the old

thing had been bestowed upon her

by a whimsical creator once Ms.

Hicks was pretty sure Aunt Wilma

meant her to understand she'd have

preferred a turtle's body if they'd

asked her at the time they were

                              giving

them out & this was when it was time

to change Aunt Wilma's diaper & turn

her & the old lady kind of flapped

her hand at the same time she pulled

in her chin so that for that instant

she looked enough like a turtle that

Ms. Hicks laughed aloud & Aunt Wilma

blinked at her so that Ms. Hicks from

that moment on stopped being

                              repulsed

by the waste Aunt Wilma generated they'd

had some vocabulary trouble until Aunt

Wilma let Ms. Hicks know it was okay to

call it *puke* & *piss* & *shit* Ms. Hicks

thought neither one of them much liked

those words but in the back room where

Aunt Wilma lived now & her death lived

there too right beside her in the bed

those chunks of language became

                              truth

itself & mostly they didn't have to say
them aloud though there was less & less
of the waste Aunt Wilma couldn't manage
more than a spoonful or two of oatmeal
with brown sugar & cream & a couple of
sips of tea with honey in it her face
more & more the same expression eager
& serious but private & earnest like she
was a schoolgirl silently memorizing

                              her

multiplication tables Ms. Hicks once
thought she saw her lips move ever so
slightly but maybe she just imagined it
& truth was she sat with Aunt Wilma so
many hours & even took to sleeping there
on a pallet beside the bed that it felt
like they were becoming the same person
like Aunt Wilma was just dissolving into
her & Ms. Hicks was doing the

                              thinking

and feeling for both of them the other
family members stayed more & more away
from them too her mother & father said
it saddened them too much to see Aunt
Wilma just fading away like she was
they could remember a time when that

woman could can ten bushels of peaches

in a day & still put a chicken dinner

on the table & Ms. Hicks's

       brothers

never said why they stayed away but

she knew it was because death scared

the wee-wee out of them & maybe they

didn't know it but Ms. Hicks did & it

made her all the more fiercely attached

to Aunt Wilma oh it disturbed her when

she'd feel how cool Aunt Wilma's skin

would get like she was practicing being

dead Ms. Hicks was constantly

        covering

up her hands arms shoulders tucking her

in again & again but it wasn't the kind

of fear that kept her useless brothers

away & it wasn't that she didn't want

her Aunt Wilma to die Aunt Wilma had

all along made her understand death was

what she yearned for one day the old

lady had said aloud out of nowhere *Not*

heaven just death please & yes she

       could

have been just trying out the words but

Ms. Hicks was right there by the bed &

so she knew Aunt Wilma had wanted her to

hear what she said & Ms. Hicks liked it

that they had that goal between them for

some reason it made everything easier Ms.

Hicks expected there'd be some churchy

talking when death did finally arrive

& she wasn't about to pick a fight

                        with

the pastor or the uncles aunts & cousins

who were inclined to insert praise Jesus

into anything they said like *Pass the salt*

praise Jesus what Aunt Wilma's saying j*ust*

death please did for Ms. Hicks was make

her ready to let all that foolishness

wash over her like rain off a duck's back

as her father had liked to advise her back

when her brothers tried to tease her

                                into

crying but now she was pretty sure they

wouldn't do that any more she felt wildly

strong this one sunny morning she'd decided

just to lie in the bed beside Aunt Wilma

because her breathing had got to be so slow

she needed to be close to her to know just

exactly when her auntie's body would change

from something alive to something dead

she'd given Aunt Wilma her bath the

night

before & put lotion on her skin all over &

brushed her hair & made it look nice & when

she saw Aunt Wilma's face this morning she'd

known it was just about to happen the way

her eyelids had released themselves down

over her eyes excusing those eyes from ever

wanting or having to look at the world any

more it made perfect sense to Ms. Hicks &

she knew it wouldn't to anybody else

who

saw them in that bed together that that's

where she needed to be it wasn't even

anything she had to think about she didn't

pause even a second after the thought came

to her & she told herself she'd never confess

to anybody as long as she lived that if she

could've had her way she'd have gone right

over with Aunt Wilma she'd have stayed with

her wherever it was she was about to go.

Acknowledgments

The authors wish to thank the Jackson Center for Creative Writing at Hollins University and the following publications in which versions of these poems have previously appeared:

Blackbird (v15n1, spring 2016): "Not Heaven, Just Death, Please," "Wrangling the Recycle Bin," "What if You Are Honest," "Ms. Hicks in Spring Again," "Before Swallows Flew Into Ms. Hicks's," "Ms. Hicks Does Not Believe," "One Time Ms. Hicks Saw Somebody Die."

Los Angeles Review of Books: "Between Ms. Hicks and Her Body."

Verse-Virtual (April 2018)*:* "Why Ms. Hicks Neither Wastes Nor Minces."

Additionally, "Ms. Forgiveness" has appeared in slightly different forms in the chapbook *Anywhere You're Going* (2016) published by RIDE Solutions as part of the Art by Bus Program in Roanoke, Virginia, and in Carilion Clinic's "Poems in the Waiting Room."

This book was designed and set in Palatino Linotype by RHWD In-
dustries

Front cover design by Arne Weingart

Photograph of David Huddle by Molly Huddle

Photograph of Meighan Sharp by Michael Shuman

Printed by Salem Printing

groundhog
POETRY PRESS